Pachelbel

Canon in D

Cover photography: Copyright © 1999 Randall Wallace
All Rights Reserved

Project editor: Peter Pickow

Speed • Pitch • Balance • Loop

To access companion recorded audio and midi files online, visit:
www.halleonard.com/mylibrary

"Enter Code"
3214-0394-3173-8146

ISBN 978-0-8256-1751-5

Copyright © 1999 by Amsco Publications
International Copyright Secured All Rights Reserved

No part of this publication may be reproduced in any form or by
any means without the prior written permission of the Publisher.

Visit Hal Leonard Online at
www.halleonard.com

Contact us:
Hal Leonard
7777 West Bluemound Road
Milwaukee, WI 53213
Email: info@halleonard.com

In Europe, contact:
Hal Leonard Europe Limited
42 Wigmore Street
Marylebone, London, W1U 2RN
Email: info@halleonardeurope.com

In Australia, contact:
Hal Leonard Australia Pty. Ltd.
4 Lentara Court
Cheltenham, Victoria, 3192 Australia
Email: info@halleonard.com.au

Canon in D

Johann Pachelbel

Andante (♩ = 72)

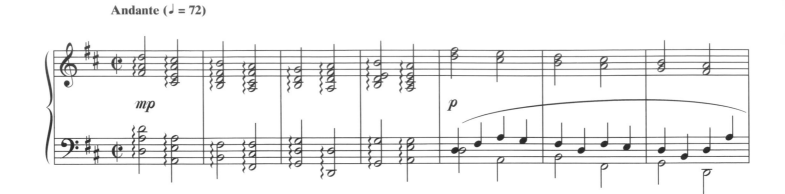

Copyright © 1999 by Amsco Publications, A Division of Music Sales Corporation.
All Rights Reserved. International Copyright Secured.

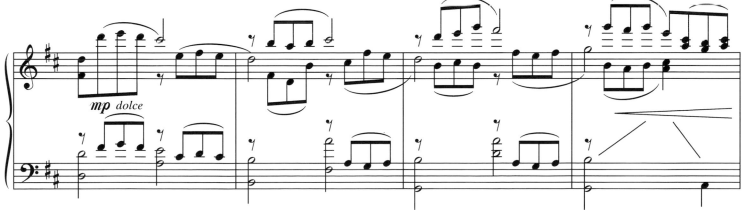

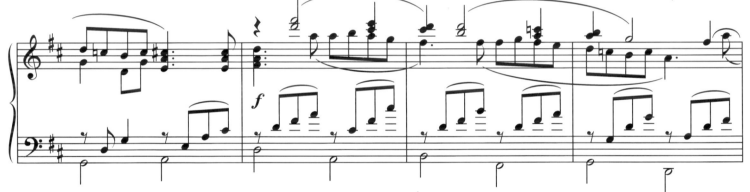